Associational Churchmanship

Recovering *our* Confessional Heritage #2

Recovering *our* Confessional Heritage

James M. Renihan, Editor-in-Chief
Richard C. Barcellos, Managing Editor

Arden L. Hodgins, Jr., *A Defense of Confessionalism: Biblical Foundations & Confessional Considerations*
James M. Renihan, *Associational Churchmanship: Second London Confession of Faith 26.12-15*

Associational Churchmanship
Second London Confession of Faith
26.12-15
James M. Renihan

The Institute of Reformed Baptist Studies
Printed by RBAP, Palmdale, CA

Requests for information should be sent to:

RBAP
349 Sunrise Terrace
Palmdale, CA 93551
rb@rbap.net
www.rbap.net

Printed in the United States of America.

Cover design and formatted for print by Cameron Porter.
Front cover Confession text was captured and graphically
modified from document excerpts at Columbia University
Libraries: https://clio.columbia.edu/catalog/4540105.

ISBN-13: 978-0-9760039-8-4
ISBN-10: 0-9760039-8-8

Endorsements

In a time when the visible church of Jesus Christ is considered irrelevant by modern society and many Evangelicals view denominations and ecclesiastical associations as too restrictive, this treatise on associational churchmanship is more needed than ever. Dr. James M. Renihan has written invaluable material that every serious Christian who loves Jesus, and the object Jesus loves most—the church—should read, study, and put into practice. This work is scholarly and simultaneously very practical. Apply what is written, and God will be glorified and Christ's kingdom will be enriched and extended.

Earl M. Blackburn
Senior Pastor
Heritage Baptist Church
Shreveport, Louisiana
****

Dr. Renihan's condensed work on chapter 26 of the Second London Confession of Faith of 1677/89 provides an excellent primer on Baptist ecclesiology. Whilst other church traditions may employ *descending* (Episcopal) or *ascending*

(Presbyterian) hierarchies to promote interchurch relationships, Dr. Renihan explains how Baptist churches have developed *reciprocal* and *cooperative* relationships for the good and prosperity of all the churches of Christ. Baptists are to be truly independent but not isolated. This volume provides historical context, gleans theological insights from the Second London Confession, and explains practical out-workings of Baptist Associations. Dr. Renihan writes with warmth, experience, and a genuine concern for biblical churchmanship. Pastors and church members alike will benefit from the volume's accessibility and noble challenge. In a time of ecclesiological indifference or isolation, we need to recover biblical principles and practices that better reflect the beauty of Christ's bride. I warmly commend this work to all who love Christ and his church, and desire to see more congregations faithfully conformed to God's word.

Michael Prodigalidad, Ph.D.
Pastor, Stanmore Baptist Church
Sydney, NSW, Australia
****

Table of Contents

Series Preface

The purpose of the series *Recovering our Confessional Heritage* is to address issues related to the Second London Confession of Faith of 1677/89 (2LCF). This centuries old Confession is widely recognized as the most important Confession of Faith in Baptist history. First published in England in 1677, it became the standard for Baptists in Colonial America through the publication of the Philadelphia (1742), Ketockton, Virginia (1766), Charleston, South Carolina, Warren, Rhode Island (both 1767), and many other editions of the Confession. As late as 1881, William Cathcart, the editor of *The Baptist Encyclopedia*, could say, "In England and America, churches, individuals, and Associations, with clear minds, with hearts full of love for the truth, . . . have held with veneration the articles of 1689." Since then, it has been adopted by Baptists around the world and translated into many languages.

We believe that, due to two factors, producing a series of short books on the 2LCF will be useful to many pastors and church members. First, there has been increased interest in the 2LCF in the first decade and a half of the twenty-first century. In fact, from the early 1960s, a greater awareness of this Confession among Baptists in the United States and around the world is evident. One of the encouraging proofs of this growing attention is the multiplication of churches who identify the 2LCF as their confessional standard.

Second, there are many issues related to the Confession that need to be clearly and cogently explained in order for an informed and robust recovery of Baptist confessionalism to continue. While churches and individuals have formally adopted the 2LCF as a standard, it has not always been clear that its contents have been fully or properly understood. As a result, the goal of this series is to aid those considering the 2LCF, as well as those already committed to it, in order to produce or maintain an informed and vigorous Baptist confessionalism.

The series will include treatments of various subjects by multiple authors. The subjects to be covered are those the series editors (along with consultants) determine to be of particular interest in our day. The authors will be those who display ample ability to address the issue under discussion. Some of the installments will be more involved than others due to the nature of the subject addressed and perceived current needs. Many of the contributions will cover foundational aspects of the self-consistent theological system expressed in the Confession. Others will address difficult, often misunderstood, or even denied facets of the doctrinal formulations of the 2LCF. Each installment will have a "For Further Reading" bibliography at the end to encourage further study on the issue discussed.

It is hoped that, by the blessing of God, these brief books will produce a better understanding of "the faith which was once for all delivered to the saints"

(Jude 3, NKJV) as well as a clearer and more robust understanding of what it means to confess the 2LCF in the twenty-first century.

James M. Renihan, Editor-in-Chief
Richard C. Barcellos, Managing Editor
October 2016

Acknowledgements

The series *Recovering our Confessional Heritage* is sponsored by the Institute of Reformed Baptist Studies in cooperation with Reformed Baptist Academic Press. The Institute of Reformed Baptist Studies is a graduate theological school which aids churches in preparing men to serve in the Gospel Ministry. For more information please visit *irbsseminary.org*.

Many thanks to Dr. Richard Barcellos for both the idea and implementation of this new series of books. We hope that they will be of great usefulness to many.

This booklet is a revised version of an address delivered at the General Assembly of the Association of Reformed Baptist Churches of America held at Grace Reformed Baptist Church, Rockford, Illinois, in April 2016.

James M. Renihan

1.

Introduction:

Three Ways to Describe

Interchurch Relations

Theology does not occur in a vacuum. It develops out of real-life situations. Men study the Word of God, contemplate its teaching, and express their conclusions. Often it is the circumstances of life that force them to think more closely and clearly about their doctrinal views and that sharpen the expressions of truth. When Arius challenged the divinity of Christ, Christians faced new questions, and the result of the debate was a clearer view of the deity of our Savior. We could give many illustrations from the history of the Church of that increasing clarity and understanding in the Creeds and Confessions of Christianity.

The doctrine of associational churchmanship expressed in our Confession is another one of these circumstances. Our discussion will involve the following: first, the three ways to describe interchurch relations; second, the church in the Second London Confession (2LCF); third, an overview of chapter 26.1-11 and brief exposition of 26.12-13; fourth associationalism; and finally, a conclusion and application. Before we actually come to look at the text of the Confession, it will be helpful for us to think about this by way of introduction to our study.

Three Ways to Describe Interchurch Relations

This is a generalization, but there are three basic views of interchurch relations, and it is good for us to recognize them. In a brief overview, we will mention Episcopacy, Presbytery, and Independency.

1. Episcopacy

Episcopacy would have been the dominant theory of interchurch relations throughout the Middle Ages and, in England, throughout the post-Reformation era up to the end of the seventeenth century. Episcopacy is a system of *descending* church power that is centered on *bishops*. The bishops stand in a position as personal representatives of Christ and they exercise authority over a particular geographic area. All the way back in the history of the early church, Cyprian, one of the bishops of North Africa, is famous for his little phrase, "No bishop, no church." If there is no bishop, then there is no real church, so that in this approach, the church is centered on the bishop. Usually, the area of authority is geographic, and all of the clergy and congregations within the *diocese* (the term used to describe the geographical area over which the bishop presides) are subject to the bishops. It is a top-down system of interchurch relationships. The bishop has the right and the authority to impose his will on those who are under him. In England, there was a system of episcopacy in which bishops had responsibility for geographic areas and had the right to impose their will upon the clergy and congregations underneath them.

2. Presbytery

Out of Geneva arose a system we know as *presbytery*. Presbytery, unlike episcopacy, is a system of *ascending* church power; church power that starts at the bottom and rises to the top. It is centered in the rule of *elders* in the church—not Bishops (in the Episcopalian sense), but elders. It starts in the congregation. The congregation elects those who will represent it in the *Session*, which has responsibility for the local congregation. The session has a direct relationship to the *presbytery*, which is the combined elders in a particular geographic area. Then in the older form (which doesn't seem to be commonly practiced anymore in America), the presbytery participated in the next highest level, the *Synod*, which typically was a grouping of presbyteries occupying a larger geographical area than any single presbytery. Finally, the synods were subject to the *General Assembly* of the Presbyterian church, so you had an ascending view of the relationship of churches that centered on eldership. Each lower court, starting with the congregation, then to the session, the presbytery, the synod, and the general assembly had the right to make its own decisions, but these decisions made by the lower court were subject to review and change by the higher court.

Some people have suggested that the American system of justice reflects a Presbyterian view of the church because there were Presbyterians who were involved in the Constitutional Convention in the 1780s, leading to its formation. Whether or not that is true, at least there is an analogous relationship between the American system of governance and the Presbyterian system. The lesser body is subject to the decisions of the higher body and the final authority is the decision of the elders who are gathered together in general assembly.

In both of these systems, episcopacy and presbytery, the visible church consists of the combined congregations, the ministers and the members, and may rightly be called a church. So you have, for example, the Roman Catholic Church, which is an episcopalian system, or you have the Protestant Episcopal Church in the United States of America. This is also the reason why we have the Presbyterian Church in America and the Orthodox Presbyterian Church. Whether epsicopalian or presbyterian, according to their principles, these bodies consider themselves, in a formal sense, a church.

I have a friend who is a long-time minister in a Reformed denomination, and he occasionally refers to the Association of Reformed Baptist Churches of America (ARBCA) as the "Reformed Baptist Church." Every time, I have to say, "No, this is not a church! We have churches, but ARBCA is not a church." It is very difficult for our Presbyterian and Episcopalian brothers to understand that point, no matter how often we tell them. You see, the local congregation called the Orthodox Presbyterian Church in any town or city is a part of the Orthodox Presbyterian Church in America. The one is a church and the other is a church, according to their system. In all of these cases, the entire body is as much a church as the individual congregation.

3. Independency

In episcopacy, you have a descending system of church power, and in the Presbyterian system, you have an ascending system of church power, but the third system is different, because the third system, which we will call independency, defines *church* as a local congregation and refuses to acknowledge anything greater as a church. The only churches are the churches represented, the churches locally from various places. Rather than independency being a system of descending or ascending power, it is a system of *reciprocating*, or perhaps *cooperating*, power, because this system views all participating churches in an equal light, with equal status, and equal rights. The church in this system can only be the local congregation. So you have episcopacy and presbytery, which ultimately form one large church, but you have independency which recognizes various churches and equates them in status and in rights.

Why is this important for us to know? Well, simply because the independent system and some of its emphases developed in response to these historical ecclesiastical circumstances. This is especially true of episcopacy, which was, until 1688 (the year of the Glorious Revolution, when William and Mary came to the throne) a persecuting, authoritarian ecclesiastical system. Our system developed in response to that system.

2.

The Church in the Context of the Second London Confession of Faith

With the three ways to describe interchurch relations in mind (and they will take on significance as we move forward), I want to begin to discuss what our Confession says about associationalism. We will notice chapter 26, especially paragraphs 14 and 15. In order to understand fully, here is the text (with modernized spelling). We will make reference to the Confession throughout the rest of our analysis.

The Text of the Confession

CHAP. XXVI.
Of the Church.

1. The Catholic or universal Church, which (with respect to the internal work of the Spirit, and truth of grace) may be called invisible, consists of the whole (*a*) number of the Elect, that have been, are, or shall be gathered into one, under Christ the head thereof; and is the spouse, the body, the fullness of him that filleth all in all.

a Heb. 12.23. Col. 1.18. Eph. 1.10,22,23. & ch. 5.23,27,32.

2. All persons throughout the world, professing the faith of the Gospel, and obedience unto God by Christ, according unto it; not destroying their own profession by any Errors everting the foundation, or unholyness of conversation, (*b*) are and may be called visible Saints; (*c*) and of such ought all particular Congregations to be constituted.

b 1 Cor. 1 2. Acts 11.26.
c Rom. 1.7. Eph. 1.20,21,22.

3. The purest Churches under heaven are subject (*d*) to mixture, and error; and some have so degenerated as to become (*e*) no Churches of Christ, but Synagogues of Satan; nevertheless Christ always hath had, and ever shall have a (*f*) Kingdome in this world, to the end thereof, of such as believe in him, and make profession of his Name.

d 1 Cor. 15. Rev. 2. & ch. 3.

e Rev. 18.2. 2 Thess. 2.11,12.

f Matt. 16.18. Ps. 72.17. & Ps. 102.28. Rev. 12.17.

4. The Lord Jesus Christ is the Head of the Church, in whom by the appointment of the Father, (*g*) all power for the calling, institution, order, or Government of the Church, is invested in a supreme & sovereign manner, neither can the Pope of *Rome* in any sense be head thereof, but is (*h*) that Antichrist, that Man of sin, and Son of perdition, that exalteth himself in the Church against Christ, and all that is called God; whom the Lord shall destroy with the brightness of his coming.

g Col. 1.18. Matt. 28.18,19,20. Eph. 4.11,12.

h 2 Thess. 2.3-9.

5. In the execution of this power wherewith he is so intrusted, the Lord Jesus calleth out of the World unto himself, through the Ministry of his word, by his Spirit, (*i*) those that are given unto him by his Father; that they may walk before him in all the (*k*) ways of obedience, which he prescribeth to them in his Word. Those thus called he commandeth to walk together in particular societies, or (*l*) Churches, for their mutual edification; and the due performance of that public worship, which he requireth of them in the World.

i Joh 10.16. chap. 12.32.

k Matt. 28.20.

l Matt. 18.15-20.

6. The Members of these Churches are (*m*) Saints by calling, visibly manifesting and evidencing (in and by their profession and walking) their obedience unto that call of Christ; and do willingly consent to walk together according to the

appointment of Christ, giving up themselves, to the Lord & one to another by the will of God, (*n*) in professed subjection to the Ordinances of the Gospel.

m Rom. 1.7. 1 Cor. 1.2.

n Acts 2.41,42. ch. 5.13,14. 2 Cor. 9.13.

7. To each of these Churches thus gathered, according to his mind, declared in his word, he hath given all that (*o*) power and authority, which is any way needful, for their carrying on that order in worship, and discipline, which he hath instituted for them to observe; with commands, and rules, for the due and right exerting, and executing of that power.

o Matt. 18.17,18. 1 Cor. 5.4,5. with v.13. 2 Cor. 2.6,7,8.

8. A particular Church gathered, and completely Organized, according to the mind of Christ, consists of Officers, and Members; And the Officers appointed by *Christ* to be chosen and set apart by the Church (so called and gathered) for the peculiar Administration of Ordinances,

and Execution of Power, or Duty, which he intrusts them with, or calls them to, to be continued to the end of the World are (*p*) Bishops or Elders and Deacons.

p Acts 20:17, with v.28. Phil. 1.1.

9. The way appointed by *Christ* for the Calling of any person, fitted, and gifted by the Holy *Spirit*, unto the Office of Bishop, or Elder, in a Church, is, that he be chosen thereunto by the common (*q*) suffrage of the Church itself; and Solemnly set apart by Fasting and Prayer, with imposition of hands of the (*r*) Eldership of the Church, if there be any before Constituted therein; And of a Deacon (*s*) that he be chosen by the like suffrage, and set apart by Prayer, and the like Imposition of hands.

q Acts 14.23: See the original.

r 1 Tim. 4.14.

s Acts 6.3,5,6.

10. The work of Pastors being constantly to attend the Service of *Christ*, in his Churches, in the Ministry of the Word, and Prayer, (*t*) with watching for their Souls, as they that must give an account

to him; it is incumbent on the Churches to whom they Minister, not only to give them all due respect, (*u*) but also to communicate to them of all their good things according to their ability, so as they may have a comfortable supply, without being themselves (*x*) entangled in Secular Affairs; and may also be capable of exercising (*y*) Hospitality toward others; and this is required by the (*z*) Law of Nature, and by the Express order of our Lord Jesus, who hath ordained that they that preach the Gospel, should live of the Gospel.

t Acts 6.4. Heb. 13.17.
u 1 Tim. 5.17,18. Gal. 6.6,7.
x 2 Tim. 2.4.
y 1 Tim. 3.2.
z 1 Cor. 9.6-14.

11. Although it be incumbent on the Bishops or Pastors of the Churches to be instant in Preaching the Word, by way of Office; yet the work of Preaching the Word, is not so peculiarly confined to them; but that others also (*a*) gifted, and fitted by the Holy *Spirit* for it, and

approved, and called by the *Church*, may
and ought to perform it.
a Acts 11.19,20,21. 1 Pet. 4.10,11.

12. As all Believers are bound to join
themselves to particular *Churches*, when
and where they have opportunity so to
do; So all that are admitted unto the
privileges of a *Church*, are also (*b*) under
the Censures and Government thereof,
according to the Rule of *Christ*.
b 1 Thess. 5.14. 2 Thess. 3.6,14,15.

13. No Church-members upon any
offence taken by them, having
performed their Duty required of them
towards the person they are offended at,
ought to disturb any *Church* order, or
absent themselves from the Assemblies
of the *Church*, or Administration of any
Ordinances, upon the account of such
offence at any of their fellow-members;
but to wait upon *Christ*, (*c*) in the further
proceeding of the *Church*.
c Matt. 18.15,16,17. Eph. 4.2,3.

14. As each *Church*, and all the Members
of it are bound to (*d*) pray continually, for

the good and prosperity of all the
Churches of *Christ*, in all places; and upon
all occasions to further it (every one
within the bounds of their places, and
callings, in the Exercise of their Gifts and
Graces) so the *Churches* (when planted by
the providence of God so as they may
enjoy opportunity and advantage for it)
ought to hold (*e*) communion amongst
themselves for their peace, increase of
love, and mutual edification.
d Eph. 6.18. Ps. 122.6.
e Rom. 16.1,2. 3 John 8,9,10.

15. In cases of difficulties or differences,
either in point of Doctrine, or
Administration; wherein either the
Churches in general are concerned, or
any one Church in their peace, union,
and edification; or any member, or
members, of any Church are injured, in
or by any proceedings in censures not
agreeable to truth, and order: it is
according to the mind of Christ, that
many Churches holding communion
together, do by their messengers meet to
consider, (*f*) and give their advice, in or
about that matter in difference, to be

reported to all the Churches concerned; howbeit these messengers assembled are not entrusted with any Church-power properly so called; or with any jurisdiction over the Churches themselves, to exercise any censures either over any Churches, or Persons: or (*g*) to impose their determination on the Churches, or Officers.

f Acts 15.2,4,6. & 22,23,25.

g 2 Cor. 1.24. 1 Joh. 4.1

The Four Major Sections of the Confession

Let's put this into context. The 2LCF includes four major sections. The first, chapters 1-6, might be called *First Principles*. It includes chapters on such foundational doctrines as Scripture, the doctrine of God, and the fall of humanity. The second division is about *The Covenant* and extends from chapter 7 through chapter 20. This segment speaks of God's covenantal purpose in saving humanity through Christ. It explains the gracious gifts God bestows on sinners. The third unit, which I call *God-centered living: Freedom and Boundaries*, contains chapters 21-30 and addresses the ways in which Christ's lordship is exercised and how believers are to live under it. The chapters on the church (26-30) are a subset of this larger segment. The final division of the Confession is the section on *The World to Come* (chapters 31-32).

3.

An Overview of Chapter 26.1-11
and Brief Exposition of 26.12-13

Chapter 26 is the first chapter in the subset
of Unit 3 dealing with the doctrine of the
church. It is the longest chapter in the
Confession, and it describes for us the
doctrine of the church in some sweeping
terms. Chapter 27 is a neglected, but very
important chapter that deals with the
Communion of Saints, especially in terms of
the obligations Christians have to each
other. Chapters 28, 29, and 30 deal with
baptism and the Lord's Supper. Chapters
26–30, on the church, are themselves a subset
of a larger section that focuses our attention

on Christian liberty. It begins in chapter 21 with a great statement about the freedom we have in Christ and then those chapters after 21, 22–30, all deal in one way or another with the question of Christian liberty. Really, it comes down to questions like, "What duties does our Lord Jesus Christ expect from his people? What are the boundaries of our liberty? Where is our freedom, and what is the boundary that is given to us in our freedom?" Chapter 26 addresses this by asserting the doctrine of the church.

An Overview of 2LCF 26.1-11

Chapter 26 develops its doctrine this way. Paragraphs 1–4 describe the invisible and visible aspects of the church of Christ. They assert that it is universal. It consists of visible saints. No individual congregation is perfect; every one of the churches described are imperfect and subject to faults. The true church never ends, and Christ alone is the Lord. In paragraph 4, it asserts that the true power in the church belongs to him, our Lord Jesus. That is why you have the statement about the Pope of Rome, because he claims blasphemously to be the authority over the church. He usurps the authority of our Lord Jesus. The central person in chapter 26 is our Lord Jesus Christ. We need to keep that in mind as we work our way through the material. It is always pointing us back to Christ and the power that belongs to him. When you see the language of lordship in chapter 26, it is a reminder of the centrality of our Lord Jesus Christ. Everything here focuses upon his will, his purpose, and what he wants to do. In fact, later on we will notice that twice in the chapter you have the phrase, "according to the mind of Christ," a very important phrase. It is in paragraph 8 and it is in one of the paragraphs at which we will look, paragraph 15.

The first section of the chapter, paragraphs 1-4, introduces and describes the church in this way. Then paragraphs 5–13 address matters of his power. How does he express his power as the central figure in the life of the church? In paragraph 5, he calls churches into being through the gospel. The assumption is that Jesus Christ, ascended to the right hand of God in heaven, is a present and active Lord who, as reigning king, calls men, women, and children to faith. He is the one who gives them faith, who causes them to believe, and who commands them to be organized together into churches.

Paragraph 6 says those who are called by his power, by the sovereign present activity of Jesus Christ, have a responsibility to join together and form local churches. Paragraph 7 says these churches, who have come into existence because Jesus Christ is Lord and is active, hold within themselves his power. He grants it to them and this power is given to the local churches; not to some higher body, not to a bishop, but it is given to the church. This is essential to the independent system; to say every church has within itself everything that is necessary to govern itself so that it does not need a higher body. It does not need the imposition of someone above it. Oftentimes we use the word *autonomy*, and on occasion that term is abused and misused. It does not mean we can thumb our noses at everybody else and claim everything belongs to us. There is a point to the doctrine of the autonomy of the church, and it is that Christ has set within the church everything it needs to accomplish his purposes for it. Of course, they have to be his purposes.

Moving on to paragraph 8, these churches are to have officers, elders (pastors, bishops) and deacons, and they are to exercise the power that is given to them. They have duties and responsibilities, and Jesus Christ has given to them power that they must exercise. In paragraph 9, our Lord Jesus Christ is directly involved in each church by giving to each of them pastors and deacons. Pastors and deacons, are Christ's gifts to the local church. This is a phrase that can be misunderstood and abused. The idea may be abused, but it is true nonetheless. When our congregations long for more officers, what we ought to do is pray to Christ and ask him to fulfill his promise to give gifts to the church so that the church will have officers. When you say, "I am Christ's gift to the church," that ought to humble you into the dust, not promote pride. It should not let you puff out your chest, but drive you to your knees and make you say, "Who am I that Jesus Christ would appoint me to the church?" That is a tremendous help to me when I have those moments of doubt and struggle and I say, "I cannot leave this behind because Christ has called me to do this. I had better fulfill my responsibility."

In paragraph 10, the duties of pastors are described to us. The meaning is clear they are to fulfill their Christ-appointed duties. They need to know what those duties are and faithfully execute them. In paragraph 11, a paragraph that thrills me to hear being brought back into practice in our churches, gifted brothers are to be recognized in our churches. We recognize that the preaching of the Word is given to some who perhaps do not occupy an office but still are called, recognized, set aside by the church, and given the authority to preach the Word of God publicly.

That is a very inadequate and rapid movement through the first 11 paragraphs, but you will notice here that there is a movement from Christ to the church and the assumption is that Jesus Christ is a present and active Lord with his church.

A Brief Exposition of 2LCF 26.12-13 (good churchmanship)

I will only deal with paragraphs 12 and 13 very briefly. They deal with good churchmanship. They speak about the way the people of God, who are the members of the church, ought to behave within the church.

All believers are required to join a local church. "As all believers are bound to join themselves to particular churches . . ." (2LCF 26.12). We saw that this doctrine is stated earlier on in the chapter (2LCF 26.2). Chapter 26.12 continues:

> . . . when and where they have opportunity so to do; so all that are admitted unto the privileges of a church, are also under the censures and government thereof, according to the rule of Christ. (2LCF 26.12)

It is not the *mind* of Christ here, as in 26.8, but the *rule* of Christ, a very similar statement. All believers are to join churches and are subject to the discipline of their churches. None of us are exempt. We are all subject to the correction of our churches should we violate the principles of the Christian life and the Christian faith.

Chapter 26, paragraph 13, says if there is a problem that arises:

> No church members, upon any offence taken by them, having performed their duty required of them towards the person they are offended at, ought to disturb any church-order, or absent themselves from the assemblies of the church, or administration of any ordinances, upon the account of such offence at any of their fellow members, but to wait upon Christ, in the further proceeding of the church.

O, that God's people would understand and practice this! Do you understand what it says? It declares that if somebody offends you, you go and do your duty according to what our Lord Jesus says. You go to that person privately and address him or her and you hope to win that person over as your brother. You hope that is the end of it, but if he or she does not respond properly, you take one or two others with you and you go so that the matter escalates. Finally, it comes before the church. Rather than getting in a huff and walking off, you wait. Notice the very end: ". . . wait upon Christ . . ." Here is the assumption again that Jesus Christ is a present and active Lord in the church. This is something I have tried to cultivate in my own mind as a pastor.

Sometimes men who serve alone in churches, as single elders, feel as if they are alone, but they are not really. Do you know why? It is because Jesus Christ is each one's co-pastor. He is the Good Shepherd and he loves your church. He gave himself for each church and he is truly spiritually present in the church. He speaks to you through his Word and tells you what your duty is. We are not talking about something mystical here, but Jesus Christ is present and all of our people need to learn that his presence can be trusted.

One of the realities of our Lord Jesus is that he is gentle, kind, and patient with sinners. Sometimes we are aggressive and we want answers. We want people to be dealt with immediately, but the Lord Jesus says, "Hold on. Give them an opportunity to turn away from their sin and repent." That is what this is saying. Good churchmanship does not walk off in dismay, saying, "Things are not going the way I want them to go. I have been offended and the church has not acted in the right way," but rather, it declares, "I will wait upon Christ." Of course, what does that mean? It means coming to him in prayer, assuming his powerful presence and activity. It means coming to him, praying to him, and asking him to work and to resolve the circumstance in the further proceeding of the church as this escalates and moves forward in the action of the church. Ultimately, it is the church that will make a determination about what happens. These paragraphs give us a context of proper churchmanship, and we will come back to this at the end, remembering this model of how individuals are to behave in their circumstances in a church.

4.

Associationalism:

Chapter 26.14-15

Paragraphs 14 and 15 conclude chapter 26 by addressing the matter of the interrelationship of churches, and they do this in a Baptist form. Much of the material of chapter 26 comes from two documents. One was the Savoy Declaration, which was the Congregationalists' revised version of the Westminster Confession of the Presbyterians from the 1640s. The Savoy Congregationalists also published, alongside of their Confession, what was called the Platform of Polity, a series of statements that described how churches were to function. In this case, paragraphs 14 and 15 are taken directly from the Savoy Platform of Polity with some subtle modifications that better fit the practices of Baptist associationalism as over against early Congregational polity. As an example, we should notice one phrase removed by the Baptists. The Savoyans state that the elders meet together in a synod, and Thomas Goodwin, one of the key members of the Savoy Synod, indicates that the synod has the right and jurisdiction over the congregational churches.[1] Our fathers

---

[1] Thomas Goodwin and Philip Nye wrote, citing John Cotton: "And because these particular congregations, both elders and people, may disagree and miscarry, and abuse this power committed to them; he [i.e. Cotton] therefore, secondly, asserteth an association or communion of churches sending their elders and messengers into a synod, (so he purposely chooseth to style those assemblies of elders, which the reformed churches do call classes or presbyteries, that so he might distinguish them from those presbyteries of congregations before mentioned) and acknowledges that it is an ordinance of Christ, unto whom Christ hath (in relation to rectifying

removed that, because even in their early Congregational polity, they did not want a higher body of any kind to have jurisdiction over the churches. This really is Baptist associationalism as understood by our fathers.

The Basic Doctrine of Associationalism: 2LCF 26.14

The way the Confession typically works is by giving the basic doctrine first and then it expresses the details of how that doctrine should work out. That is exactly what we have in chapter 26, paragraphs 14 and 15. Paragraph 14 is the basic doctrine. Notice the

---

maladministrations and healing dissentions in particular congregations, and the like cases) committed a due and just measure of power, suited and proportioned to those ends; and furnished them, not only with ability to give counsel and advice, but further upon such occasions with a ministerial power and authority to determine, declare and enjoin such things as may tend to the reducing such congregations to right and peace." Larzer Ziff, ed., *John Cotton on the Churches of New England* (Cambridge: The Belknap Press, 1968), 75-76.

language: "As each church, and all the members of it . . ." Think of your church. Just put the name of your church in there.

> As each church, and all the members of it, are bound to pray continually *for the good and prosperity of all the churches of Christ*, in all places, and upon all occasions to further *it* (every one within the bounds of their places and callings, in the exercise of their gifts and graces) so the churches (when planted by the providence of God so as they may enjoy opportunity and advantage for *it*) ought to hold communion among themselves, for their peace, increase of love, and mutual edification. (emphasis added)

Now let us look at this a little bit more closely. I will try to highlight some things and make some comments on these phrases. In this paragraph, we are first presented with a universal obligation. Notice the language here of *all places*: ". . . each church, and all the members of it, are bound to pray continually for the good and prosperity of all the churches of Christ, in all places . . ."

We have a universal obligation that belongs to each church. Remember, I said put in the name of your church. Your church has an obligation for the good and prosperity of all the churches of Christ in all places. I hope you pray for other churches in your community. Maybe they are not Reformed Baptist churches, but if they are true churches, you ought to pray for them. You ought to pray for the churches in your state, the United States, and around the world, for God's movement in their midst on the Lord's Day. Let us not be sectarian. We must recognize that there are other true churches that are not exactly like us but are still true churches. This is an exhortation within our Confession to recognize that and to promote it.

It is also true of every church member. Not only is it every church (put in your church's name again), but every member of every church has this obligation in some way. Largely, all we can do is pray here. There is not much more we can do in a universal obligation for the church in all places. Nevertheless, we have this responsibility. Yet notice what it is about. It is ". . . for the good and prosperity of all the churches of Christ . . ." Ultimately, that is what associationalism is about. It is the good of the churches. *Good*, here, would have the sense that it has in a place such as the pastoral Epistles: *good* as defined by God. Not just something that culturally we look at and say, "That is a good thing," but something that is good as defined by Scripture. *Prosperity*, of course, here, does not mean wealth. It means spiritual growth. It means an increase of holiness, an increase of the extension of the gospel. That is our responsibility. A universal obligation for each church and each church member to pray for the good and prosperity of all of the churches of Christ.

Notice that I have highlighted the word *it* above: ". . . and upon all occasions to further *it* . . ." And here: ". . . as they may enjoy opportunity and advantage for *it* . . ." *It* equals "the good and prosperity of all the churches of Christ." When you read this paragraph, the antecedent of *it*, the referent of *it* must be in your minds as "the good and

prosperity of all of the churches of Christ."
We are upon all occasions to further it, to
further the good and prosperity of all the
churches of Christ. When they are planted
by the providence of God so they may enjoy
opportunity and advantage for it, "for the
good and prosperity of the churches of
Christ . . ." That is what associationalism first
and foremost is about. It is the good and
prosperity of your church, of the church of
the brother or sister in Christ who is a
member of a different congregation, of the
other church, and of another church, and
again another church, and so forth. It is
about working together, supporting and
strengthening one another so we are not
isolated and trying to go it alone in the
kingdom of God. Rather, together, we are
strengthening each other. That will have
significance as we move forward.

The next phrase I want to highlight is
interesting; notice that we have the little
word *it* occurring again. We know that to
which *it* refers; now we must notice some
specific ways *it* is to be implemented when
the text states, ". . . *every one within the bounds*

of their places and callings . . ." This phrase is an instance of the fact that sometimes language changes over the years. When you look at *boundary* and *place*, you think geographic location, don't you? That is the natural way for twenty-first-century English readers in America, and probably in other English speaking countries as well, to read this. They think, "Well, it is talking about geography," but actually, it is not.

Let me show you something else that is going on here. The phrase ". . . the bounds of their places and callings . . ." has a very specific meaning. In the *Oxford English Dictionary* on the word *place*, we find this: "A position or standing in an order of estimation or merit. Specifically, a person's social rank or status, the duty or rights appropriate to a social rank."[2] That is what the statement in the Confession has in mind here. It is thinking especially of the church and the fact that there are some ranks (not social) within the church. Do you know what we call them? We call them elders,

---

[2] *Oxford English Dictionary*, s.v. "place."

deacons, and members. That is what this is talking about. It is saying to us that there are different responsibilities that the people in the church have according to the bounds of their places.

Let me give you a couple of illustrations of how this works in religious literature. The Solemn League and Covenant from 1643 was the agreement between the Scots and the English to work together in the civil war against King Charles I. In the Solemn League and Covenant, we read:

> We shall also, according to our places and callings, in this common cause of religion, liberty, and peace of the kingdoms, assist and defend all those that enter into this League and Covenant, in the maintaining and pursuing thereof . . .[3]

Of course, here they are talking about social ranks. Those who are higher in the social

---

[3] *A Solemn League and Covenant for Reformation, and Defence of Religion* (Edinburgh: Robert Bryson, 1643), 6.

Associationalism: Chapter 26.14-15

system, as they give themselves to the Solemn League and Covenant, commit themselves to use their resources and their status in society to further the cause of religion as over against the English king. Here we have the same language used very clearly with regard, not to geography, but to one's position in a particular society.

In an interesting sermon by Robert Sanderson on Proverbs 24:10–12 from 1630, he says:

> The truth is there is an outward and there is an inward honor. The outward honor belongeth immediately to the place and the place casteth it upon the person so that whatsoever person holdeth the place, it is meet he should have the honor due to the place, whether he deserve it or not.[4]

If this were in the secular realm, it would be someone who is in the ranks of nobility, an earl or a duke. Maybe the man is a good

---

[4] *Sermons, by the Right Reverend Father in God, Robert Sanderson* (London: All. Arnold and Co., 1841 reprint), 412.

leader in his community. We honor him for this. Maybe he isn't, but still, because he has that place, we show him honor. When this is applied to the church, it means pastors and deacons need to be given the proper honor that they rightly deserve because of the office they hold.

Again, I do not mean any political overtones to this, but if the President of the United States walked into the room, whatever we thought of his policies, it would be right for us to honor him because of the office he holds. In a sense, that is what this is about. It is what our Confession is addressing—the fact that there are bounds of places and calling. It has specific meaning and it refers to a rank and position in a society. In this case, it is the rank and position one has in the church. So let's read it with this meaning:

> As each church, and all the members of it, are bound to pray continually for the good and prosperity of all the churches of Christ, in all places, and upon all occasions to further it (every one within the bounds of their places and callings…)

Associationalism: Chapter 26.14-15

Different people, according to the positions they hold, have different responsibilities in the furtherance of the good and prosperity of all the churches of Christ.

This is ". . . in the exercise of their gifts and graces . . ." This again has specific meaning. We need to be precise and we need to think about what it says. Each one, according to the place and calling, exercises gifts and graces. To summarize, pastors, gifted brothers, deacons, and members have obligations for the good and prosperity of the churches of Christ, but the requirements are not all the same. Not everyone does the same things. They are not the same obligations. Pastors, gifted brothers, and deacons use their office-gifts to increase the good and prosperity of the church. Notice how "gifts and graces" are employed in the Confession. When it speaks of *gifts*, it means those who hold office in the church and have spiritual gifts to use. When it is talking about *graces*, it refers to holiness in the life of all of the people. The gifts in the church are the pastors, gifted brothers, and deacons. They use their gifts specifically for the good and prosperity of all of the churches, and additionally everyone employs their graces so that all pray and give as God gives them ability, in order to increase the good and prosperity of the churches. This is a kingdom perspective. You see, it is everybody in the church recognizing that they have a part, a role to play in the forward movement, not only of their own church, but in the good and benefit that is extended to all of the rest of the churches as well.

In ARBCA, there are no individual members. It has churches who are in membership, but all of the members of each member church are members of ARBCA. They really are! They are members of ARBCA. Not that they have an individual membership in the association, but because their churches participate, they also participate, and for this reason they have obligations. Those obligations are the good and prosperity of all of the churches of Christ. As we will see, it gets even more specific as we move ahead.

When *providence* affords *opportunity* and *advantage*, the churches together are to advance *it*, that is, the "good and prosperity of all of the churches." How do they do this when providence affords opportunity and advantage? Well, what does it mean by "providence affording opportunity and advantage"? Churches, with the ability to work together to advance this cause, "ought to hold communion among themselves." This is associationalism. That is what our Confession is teaching here. The good and the prosperity of the churches is advanced by means of the ought-ness, the *necessity*, of holding communion among themselves.

Now, there are some of our brothers who do not approve of our doctrine of associationalism who want to read *communion* as if it means the friendship of pastors. We do not have the time to go into this. Let me give you a summarizing quotation from my book, *Edification and Beauty*, which was my Ph.D. dissertation. The final chapter deals with the meaning of the word *communion*. I argue at length in there that *communion* is the equivalent of association. The recent book, *Faith and Life for Baptists*, illustrates how our confessional

Particular Baptist fathers move back and forth using the language of *associate* or *association* when they refer to what they are.[5] Here is the final quotation from my dissertation.

> The weight of this evidence provides strong indication that the final paragraphs of chapter 26 of the Second London Confession advocate formal association in their use of the word *communion*. From the beginning of the movement in the 1640s, the established pattern of interchurch relationships points to this fact. Among the Baptists, and even at times among the Independents, the word was used in a technical sense, referring to formal associations.[6]

---

[5] See James M. Renihan, ed., *Faith and Life for Baptists: The Documents of the London Particular Baptist General Assemblies, 1689-94* (Palmdale, CA: RBAP, 2016).

[6] James M. Renihan, *Edification and Beauty: The Practical Ecclesiology of the English Particular Baptists, 1675-1705* (Milton Keynes, UK: Paternoster, 2008), 172.

When we read in the paragraph of the Confession that they "ought to hold communion," this means they ought to form associations of churches. That is the only proper sense that can be given to it. Notice, ". . . when planted by the providence of God so as they may enjoy opportunity . . ." There may be places where churches are so isolated they cannot enter into communion with others. It is not a requirement except when the providence of God makes it possible. The providence of God has made it possible in many places. ARBCA is a national association of churches. There are several regional associations of churches in the United States and Canada. There is an association of Reformed Baptist churches in New Zealand. That is the providence of God bringing churches together.

Notice at the end of paragraph 14 that this notion of the good and prosperity of all of the churches of Christ is repeated using alternate language. Now we read about the "peace, increase of love, and mutual edification," a further definition that is given to the notion of good and prosperity. It is so that the churches, individually and collectively, might have peace, that love might grow within the church and among the churches, and that they might be edified. So we have at the beginning and at the end of this paragraph these parallel statements which define for us the nature of the good and the prosperity of all of the churches. It is peace, increase of love, and mutual edification.

Let's summarize what we see from chapter 26, paragraph 14. There are universal obligations. We ought to pray. We ought to further the good and prosperity of the churches. There are providential obligations that depend upon our places and bounds—gifts and graces. The gifts are pastors, gifted brothers, and deacons, and they ought to use their gifts for the good of the larger community of churches. Graces are to be exercised by everyone. Associationalism is a providential duty, and the goal of this is the good and prosperity of the churches, peace, increase of love, and mutual edification. Churches care for and aid other churches in associations. That is what the doctrine is here. That is what associationalism is about. It is caring for and aiding other churches.

The Basic Practice of Associationalism: 2LCF 26.15

Paragraph 15 of chapter 26 provides the details of associationalism, the how-to, so let us read it again.

> In cases of difficulties or differences, either in point of doctrine or administration, wherein either the churches in general are concerned, or any one church, in their peace, union, and edification; or any member or members of any church are injured, in or by any proceedings in censures not agreeable to truth and order: it is according to the mind of Christ, that many churches holding communion together, do, by their messengers, meet to consider, and give their advice in or about that matter in difference, to be reported to all the churches concerned; howbeit these messengers assembled, are not intrusted

with any church-power properly so called; or with any jurisdiction over the churches themselves, to exercise any censures either over any churches or persons; or to impose their determination on the churches or officers.

This is a fairly comprehensive statement. Sometimes we miss the full teaching that is incorporated here. Not only is this true of some doctrines in the Confession, but it is also true of this practical paragraph as well. Confessionalism calls us humbly to listen and perhaps revise our practice according to what our Confession states. The presupposition of this paragraph is the phrase, "according to the mind of Christ." For the sake of time, I will pass over this, but in paragraph 8, you also have this phrase, "according to the mind of Christ." It simply means this is the stated will of Jesus Christ for his churches, that they work together for the good and prosperity of one another, and the way of doing this is that they hold communion together. That is how it works, and of course, *communion* means forming associations of churches.

Let's examine this paragraph. We will start at the beginning. There we read: "In cases of difficulties or differences, either in point of doctrine or administration . . ." We need to look at this very closely and think about it carefully. I am going to argue that there are four things that are laid out for us here. I will be redundant in order to be able to make the point. The first two things we encounter are *difficulties* in doctrine and *difficulties* in administration, and then we have *differences* in doctrine and *differences* in administration. We have four things that are set our before us. There are four possibilities that associationalism addresses: 1) difficulties in doctrine; 2) difficulties in administration; 3) differences in doctrine; and 4) differences in administration.

What is this about? Let me give some examples. One example of a difficulty in doctrine that was encountered by our brothers in the seventeenth century was the question of justification from eternity. In the narrative of the 1689 Assembly, we read that the 1689 General Assembly had to address this. This was an increasing problem that, later on in the 1690s, actually erupted into a church split. At this point, in 1689, they are discussing and trying to work their way through what is a very difficult question of doctrine and the result is that they reject it. The 2016 ARBCA General Assembly (GA) had some examples of the difficulties in doctrine by some of its discussions. For example, there was a draft proposal for the discussion of subscription which was discussed, specifically concerning the wording of terms related to our documents. Is it subscription to all of them? Is it affirmation? Is it adherence? That discussion was seeking to resolve a difficulty in doctrine. The GA was not settling the doctrine. It was simply trying to work through how that expresses itself.

What about difficulties in administration that ought to come before associations? Well, there is the question of ministerial support and the question of ministerial training, which were both present at the 1689 General Assembly. At the 2016 ARBCA

Associationalism: Chapter 26.14-15

GA, my co-elder and I proposed a question to the assembly about whether or not pastors ought to be aware of the amount of money their people give in their offerings. That was a genuine question on our part because we wanted to hear the wisdom of others. I was really helped by that conversation. It gave me some information and confirmed, in many ways, what we have done in the past. I was thankful for that. That was a difficulty in administration that was discussed among the churches and it helped us to be able to move forward in the conclusions made. That is an example of what the Confession is talking about. It is a difficulty in administration. How should we as elders administer this action in our church? I found it tremendously helpful.

You see, sometimes when we read this, we only think about bad things, but it is actually addressing the possibility of helping us with good things. The discussion mentioned above, which addressed several subsidiary questions, was incredibly helpful. Several of those present indicated they were helped by the comments of the men. That is a good example of what this is talking about.

What about differences in doctrine? Well, should a church worship on the first day or the seventh day? That was a question that faced the 1689 General Assembly, and their resolution was that the day has been changed and we worship the triune God on the first day of the week, not on the seventh day. In their case, they had to exclude a seventh-day church from participation as a result. This is a difference in doctrine. Apparently, when considering this seventh-day church, there would have been agreement on the rest of the confessional issues, but not about the day when Christian churches gather to worship. After discussion, the 1689 General Assembly said, "That day is important. We will not give in on that."

What about differences in administration? Well, one of the questions asked was, "How do you recover people who have wrongly left the church?" How do we recover these people? Or, what about the maladministration of church discipline? (We will see this again in a moment.) Those are just examples of the four possibilities.

The doctrine also says that these things may occur among the churches in general (that is, the churches in the association) or they may affect one church "in their peace, union, and edification." This language largely reflects the earlier expression of paragraph 14. Do you see how this is all woven together? These problems, these four possibilities may occur among churches, they may occur in one church, they may affect one member of a church, or they may affect two or more members. I do not know how precisely to quantify "members" beyond "two or more." It is just plural, thus it is two or more members. If they are members of any church, if they are injured by unjust censures or proceedings not agreeable to the truth, they have a means of protection. This is the doctrine of associational protection.

The statement in the Confession contemplates many churches and one church, and many members, and one member of one church. The way I think about it is by imagining a camera on a satellite looking down at a particular place on the surface of the earth. At first it might view a region, then it zeroes in on a neighborhood, and then it zeroes in on a house, and then it zeroes in on one person in that house. The Confession contemplates all of those possibilities and allows for recourse in the case of problems — differences in doctrine and administration and difficulties in doctrine and administration. Many churches may have these, or one church may have any of these, or even one member or two or more members of any church. It moves from the larger to the smaller like a satellite zooming in on more specific areas. This is associational protection for one member, two or more members, or even for a church. That is what the association is intended to do.

Notice the content: spiritual injuries, censures against truth (of course, that would refer especially to false witnesses as they are presented in Scripture), or censures against order. Someone like Diotrephes comes to mind, who exercises authority in ways in which he ought not. It is of "the mind of Christ, that many churches holding communion together, do, by their messengers, meet to consider, and give their advice in or about that matter in difference, to be reported to all the churches concerned . . ." *Messengers* is a technical term for representatives of churches. Notice the messengers meet, consider, and advise. This is an important theological and practical point. It teaches us that the business of the association is done by the association. It is done by the association, not by subordinate bodies. All of the decisions of the association are a result of the consideration (notice the language) of the messengers and not anyone else.

This protects the association from committees functioning within the association as an eldership ought to function within a church. Associations of churches ought not to have any committees which act as an eldership to the association. This does not mean committees are non-confessional. Of course not, because our fathers established committees. The nine men who administered the ministerial support fund, and the seven men who examined the books about the singing controversy, were committees, but we ought to notice how these committees functioned.[7] They administered the decisions of the General Assembly, and not vice versa. They did not have legislative power; they only had administrative power. Everything came back to the General Assembly. This is clearly exemplified in the actions of their committees. According to the Confession, in 26.15, all of the churches are to receive a report of the considerations and advice of the messengers, and these are the narratives that we have available to us today. As reported in the narrative, this is the clear teaching of our Confession of Faith.

Conclusion

Let's go back to the introduction. Independency is reciprocating church

---

[7] See Renihan, ed., *Faith and Life for Baptists*, 55 and 96ff.

Associationalism: Chapter 26.14-15

power. Every church is equal in status, but does this mean the association cannot discipline itself? Well, the answer is no, it does not mean this. It can refuse commendation to churches (for example, the seventh-day church in London) or resist heresy, but it cannot and must not unchurch a church. It may exclude a congregation from its fellowship, but it cannot make pronouncements about an assembly's claim to legitimacy. It cannot say, "You are no longer a church." It cannot impose or remove officers, in contrast to what a bishop or a presbytery might do. A presbytery can remove a whole session from a local congregation. We cannot do that. It also cannot impose its advice on churches. In the Independent or Congregational system, the churches are free to take or to leave such counsel.

Episcopacy was about church power. William Laud, the Archbishop of Canterbury from 1633–1645, and then Charles II and his bishops, after he was restored to the throne from 1660–1685, imposed all kinds of offensive practices on the churches. There was the Great Ejection on St. Bartholomew's Day in 1662. There was the draconian Clarendon Code, imposed upon those who dissented from the Church. The ecclesiastical authorities had the right to impose and remove ministers. In cooperation with the magistrate, they had the right to impose fines or to imprison those who were church members.

Presbyterianism, in some of its forms, was described by John Milton in that famous poem, titled, "On the New Forcers of Conscience," under the Long Parliament, as "New presbyter is but old priest writ large." Milton meant, "the Presbyterians who are now in power are just the same as the Episcopalians who were in power previously; they want to do away with us." Independency was born in response to these and it rejects both of them.

Application

I have three things I want to say by way of application. Our Confession teaches us at least three important things, and we must do

what it requires. It requires of us
commitment, *participation*, and *preparation*.

1. Associational commitment

First, to "hold communion among
themselves" is a wonderful phrase because
it speaks to the commitment we make when
becoming part of an association. It is a
reciprocal love, friendship, and support to
cooperate together for noble goals—the
good and prosperity of all the churches,
their peace, increase of love, and mutual
edification. Yet how many of those terms
require of us mutual commitment? "All the
churches," "mutual edification," "hold
communion among themselves . . ." By
coming together, confessional associations
of churches agree to live with one another in
order to achieve those goals. It means
staying together and supporting one
another, even in decisions with which we
disagree. The Petty France, London, church
did this in 1689. Their pastor, William
Collins, signed the epistle at the beginning
of the General Assembly *Narrative* even

though the church he represented disagreed with the statement about regulators found in the *Narrative*.[8] They might have withdrawn, because in some ways that statement was targeted at them, but they did not. They held on and stayed in the association, to their credit. We will not always agree on everything we do, but we must hold onto our communion together, even when we disagree. That means humbly bowing to the will of the whole and supporting its decisions. Here we have an analogy to the churchmanship we saw in chapter 26, paragraphs 12 and 13, where the members of the church are to work together even when things do not go the way they would like them to go. They wait upon Christ in the working of the churches.

Holding communion together requires commitment through the good and through the bad. If the ARBCA GA, for example, makes a decision with which the elders of one of the churches does not agree, the

---

[8] For details, see Renihan, ed., *Faith and Life for Baptists*, 23-24.

obligation is to continue together and support one another even though we disagree in the decision that was made by the assembly. Confessional associationalism requires commitment.

2. Associational participation

Secondly, it requires participation. Once again, think about the noble goals of associationalism—the good and prosperity of all the churches, peace, love, and edification. Churches in association are bound to further its goals and to enjoy opportunity and advantage for them. So I ask associational pastors this question: What gifts do you have in your church that you can share? What can you do for the good and prosperity of all the churches? How can you share your pastors, who perhaps can preach in churches that are in need? Maybe give pulpit supply to them? There is a church in the Southern California Association of Reformed Baptist Churches that was in this circumstance for years and it was great to witness how the local associational churches came together to supply the pulpit, week after week. It is with joy that I report that the Lord has blessed that congregation with a pastor recently.

Do you have gifted brothers who could assist in other churches? Do you have deacons who can use their skills in benevolence? Is there a church nearby with an empty pulpit, or is there a lone elder who needs a break, some time away? Are there physical needs to repair a building with which your deacons and your people could aid? Do you have people who have talents they might be able to share?

A couple of years ago I visited a church. I preached there on a Sunday morning and afterwards had a conversation with the pastor about ARBCA. He asked me the question, "What benefit will the association bring to my church?" I tried to give him an honest answer to that question, but then I said to him, "Maybe you need to think about it another way. What benefits can your church bring to the association?" We live in a consumerist culture that thinks about ourselves, but in associationalism, we need

Associationalism: Chapter 26.14-15

to think about others and remember the words of the Lord Jesus Christ who said, "It is more blessed to give than to receive." That is what associationalism is. We give to others more than we receive from them.

3. Associational preparation

Thirdly, associationalism requires preparation. Paragraph 15 is about weighty matters not to be taken lightly — difficulties and differences in doctrine or administration. Associational meetings should deal with serious topics, and this requires caution and in-depth thought. The best discussions associational meetings will have and the best conclusions that will be drawn will come when careful consideration to matters is given beforehand, when ideas are weighed according to Scripture and are presented from reasoned positions. Our advantage over our fathers and our brothers is that we are much more easily able to communicate beforehand the topics to be discussed. The advice we give to one another ought to be the fruit of careful preparation governed by brotherly love.

It also means we come in humility. It is a good thing to ask for advice, to say, "We don't know if our wisdom on this issue is sufficient." So if and when you are asked to supply topics for associational discussions, do so. Give it some thought. Bring your questions. Listen to the advice of the GA. Be prepared, when a perceived injury has been suffered, to listen carefully and respond righteously. Associations, when functioning properly, assist churches in weighty matters. This deserves our best preparation, not top-of-the-head advice. Our Confession requires us to be committed, prepared participants in our association so that the good and the prosperity of the churches, their peace, love, and mutual edification, may increase. When these grow, so do the churches and the Christians in them. May God help us to be characterized by these things that we find in our Confession of Faith.

Associationalism: Chapter 26.14-15

Appendix:

Notes on 2LCF 26.14-15

2LCF Chapter 26 Paragraphs 14 & 15 Comments

14. As each Church, and all the members of it, are bound to (a) pray continually, for the good and prosperity of all the Churches of Christ, in all places; and upon all occasions to further it	**1.** This phrase implies universal obligation. Notice that the key idea is The good and prosperity of all the churches . . . . It is equivalent to peace, increase of love and mutual edification at the end of the paragraph. Notice also the use of the word it and its antecedent—. . . good and prosperity . . . .
(every one within the bounds of their places, and callings, in the Exercise of their Gifts and Graces)	**2.** The parenthetical statement limits this obligation according to place and calling. This refers to at least two things: churches and

so the Churches (when planted by the providence of God so as they may enjoy opportunity and advantage for it)	elders should not intrude themselves into other churches (under the guise of furthering the good and prosperity of the churches); and the doctrine of 26.11: God has given certain responsibilities (callings) to some men, not all in the churches. Everyone ought to pray, others should cautiously do more. See also 2LCF 20.3 and John Owen, Biblical Theology Book 1 Chapter 6.
ought to hold (b) communion	
amongst themselves	
for their peace, increase of love, and mutual edification. a. Eph. 6:18; Psalm 122:6. b. Rom. 16:1-2; 3 John 8-10.	3. This is local (providential) obligation: it is more specific. 4.Opportunity=occasion; advantage=increase. 5. Notice the second use of it. The antecedent is the same. 6. *Ought* speaks of obligation. 7. Hold communion is technical terminology equivalent to "being in association."

Notes on 2LCF 26.14-15

	8. Formal associations are limited by geography. Presbyterians argued for national churches, Independents argued for national (or more local) associations. **9.** Associations provide opportunity, in providential contexts to further the good and prosperity of the churches.
15. In cases of difficulties or differences, either in point of Doctrine, or administration; wherein either the Churches in general are concerned, or any one Church in their peace, union, and edification;	**1.** There may be difficulties in doctrine, difficulties in administration, differences in doctrine and differences in administration. **2.** These may affect churches or a church, and may have to do with three things: peace, union, and edification. These are not necessarily negative things: a difficulty of

or any member, or members of any Church are injured, in or by any proceedings in censures not agreeable to truth, and order:	administration could be a church's inability to provide suitable financial support for its pastor. **3.** Notice *or*. The issues now focus specifically on wrongs.
	4. A member or members may be injured through a miscarriage of discipline.
it is according to the mind of Christ,	**5.** Truth=right doctrine as well as the true facts of the case; order=proper
that many Churches holding communion together,	practice and procedure. **6.** Notice the assertion that Christ appoints the method prescribed.
do by their messengers meet	**7.** Notice that holding communion is an established fact. The
to consider, (c) and give their advice, in or about that matter in difference, to be reported to all the Churches concerned;	churches that are in communion (association) are to proceed. **8.** Churches are represented by messengers.
howbeit these messengers assembled, are not entrusted with any Church-power	**9.** Messengers deliberate (consider) and advise. **10.** A report of the deliberation and advice

properly so called; or with any jurisdiction over the Churches themselves, to exercise any censures either over any Churches, or persons: or (d) to impose their determination on the Churches, or Officers. c. Acts 15:2,4,6,22-23,25. d. 2 Cor. 1:24; 1Jn 4:1.	must be reported to all the churches. **11.** The messengers do not have church power or jurisdiction. They cannot censure churches or individuals—i.e. there is no presbyterial power of church discipline. **12.** Nor can they impose their conclusions on churches or officers. In this way, the determinations of the association can only be advisory.

For Further Reading

On Episcopacy:

Lightfoot, J. B. *Saint Paul's Epistle to the Philippians*. London: MacMillan, 1890. See pages 180-269. This is a classic defense of the Episcopalian form of church government.

On Presbytery:

Bannerman, James. *The Church of Christ*. Edinburgh: T&T Clark, 1868. Two Volumes. This has been reprinted by the Banner of Truth Trust. This is a classic defense of the Presbyterian form of church government.

For Baptist Associations:

Copson, Stephen. *Association Life of the Particular Baptists of Northern England,*

1699-1732. London: The Baptist Historical Society, 1991.

Gillette, A. D. *Minutes of the Philadelphia Baptist Association from A.D. 1707, to A.D. 1807; Being the First One Hundred Years of Its Existence.* Philadelphia: American Baptist Publication Society, 1851.

Renihan, James M. *Edification and Beauty: The Practical Ecclesiology of the English Particular Baptists, 1675-1705.* Milton Keynes: Paternoster, 2008. See especially chapter 6.

_____. *Faith and Life for Baptists: The Documents of the London Particular Baptist General Assemblies, 1689-94.* Palmdale, CA: RBAP, 2016.

White, B. R. *Association Records of the Particular Baptists of England, Wales and Ireland to 1660.* 3 volumes. London: The Baptist Historical Society, 1971-74.

Further Reading

CPSIA information can be obtained
at www.ICGtesting.com
Printed in the USA
FFOW03n2053120517
35398FF